First Page to Finished
On Writing and Living the Writer's Life

MARITA GOLDEN

ISBN: 979-8-218-33765-0

TABLE OF CONTENTS

INTRODUCTION

I started writing stories when I was six or seven years old. That's a long time. In these pages I'm sharing with you what I've learned and come to understand and value about writing and being a writer. We like to modify the noun writer with adjectives that we feel enhance the word. Great writer. Best-selling writer. Famous writer. But the word writer standing on its own is just fine.

Choose to become a writer and you embark on a journey that signals a desire to search for the various and varied meanings of truth, a willingness to interrogate conventional wisdom. You will call forth imagination on a continuing basis and strive to make language beautiful and thought-provoking.

I've spent most of my life becoming a writer. With each new narrative I am learning how to write. I am standing at another starting point. Writing is much more than mastering craft. Becoming a writer is mostly about imagining dangerously, writing regularly and being insatiably curious about human nature.

Remain confident in your ability to write well, work hard, and renew your allegiance to the writing life each day and you can become the writer you want to be. Believe me, I know dreams do come true.

1 FIRST WORDS

How do you begin a story? How do you invite the reader into the world you have created? The language should be seductive, concrete and yet mysterious. The reader needs to feel the pull of questions that are urgent, and immediate, questions for which they want an answer. An answer they are willing to turn the page for.

This is the opening paragraph of my novel *Long Distance Life*:

"The story of my family's no different, really, than the story of yours. I'm so old now, that every day I live is a surprise to people who think old folks die on some kinda schedule. I wish I could say I'd accumulated a whole lot of wisdom from all I've been through. I probably got a little more sense that you, just 'cause I'm so old. But even *that* depends on who *you* are.

I will say this, though, and it took me getting this old to understand why old folks said it all the time: "I'd do it all the same. Cause I know changing one thing changes it all. And you not gonna get but so much of it right-you gonna get your share of sorrow, no matter what."

This is the voice of Naomi Johnson, matriarch of a Washington, D.C family, one of the narrators of a story that spans six decades. I wanted to open the book with a voice that sounded trustworthy, experienced, honest, yet endearingly self-effacing, a voice that promised the reader a complex, complicated family story. When Naomi says that her story is no different than yours, she emphasizes the humanity she shares with the reader.

The phrases "I'd do it all the same and "you gonna get your share of sorrow no matter what," invite the reader into the unfolding of the arc of her life, and the pain she has endured. What has she done that she would do again? What have her sorrows been? How old is she? These are the questions that her words have provoked.

I could have had Naomi say, "my story is no different than yours," but this is the multi-generational narrative, and the reader needs to know that, so she says,

"The story of my family's no different, really than yours."

We are drawn to compelling individuals, but we are also

drawn to families that have been tested and challenged, and

as Naomi implies somehow got through it all.

***

This is the opening page of *Don't Play in the Sun One Woman's Journey Through the Color Complex:*

"I am ten, standing before the gilt-framed mirror over the mahogany cabinet where the silver and good china are stored. It is seven-thirty and my mother, my father, and I have finished dinner. I have washed the dishes. My parents are upstairs in their bedroom. I stand before the mirror as I do almost every night when I have the dining room to myself. My head is draped in four long silk scarves that belong to my mother.

Scarves held in place with a bobby pin at the top of my head. Scarves that are a seductive color-drenched kaleidoscope whose silk fabric kisses my brown cheeks as I imagine a White girl's hair must brush her skin-with the most awesome feeling of affirmation, beauty, and power.

Standing before that mirror I am Snow White. I am Cinderella. My short, has-to-be-straightened-with-a-hot-comb hair has disappeared. My hands, like hungry butterflies are lost in the soft, imaginary tendrils that I see with a contented stranger's eyes.

With those eyes I convince myself that I can actually see the metamorphosis of the scarves into shoulder-length and even sometimes blond hair that frames my chubby brown face and that at that, at last, makes me real.

I chose a deeply personal and in retrospect, painful memory. Standing before the mirror pretending is an act most women identify with and remember. By recreating an act of racial confusion and denial that is so charged, the reader knew from page one that they could expect a narrative that was authentic and bold in exploring taboo truths.

2 QUESTIONS AND ANSWERS

The Ten Questions A Memoir or Fictional Character Must Answer:

What are the defining moments in my relationship with my mother/father/siblings?

How did my family inspire me? Wound me? Shape me?

What are the societal factors that influenced who I became?

What in my life have I longed for most?

What was I afraid I would never have?

What lifestyle/life choice patterns I have repeated?

Who broke my heart?

Who put it back together?

What is my story about in one word?

What am I most afraid of revealing?

3 HOW TO WRITE A NOVEL

Read *War and Peace* and *Anna Karenina* by Leo Tolstoy to learn how large a canvas a novel can have and still feel intimate and brim with emotion and feeling.

Read *Anna-in-Between* by Elizabeth Nunez to witness skillful use of a restricted setting to render a complex story of a family.

Read *The Buddha in the* Attic by Julie Otsuka to hear the collective voice of a nation of people through its women.

Read *Olive Kittredge* by Elizabeth Strout to grow to care for a deeply unsympathetic character.

Read *Their Eyes Were Watching God* by Zora Neale Hurston to learn how to create dynamic and unforgettable dialogue.

As you write your novel remember:

The novel you complete is not the novel you thought you would write.

The novel will and is supposed to constantly surprise you.

The novel will teach you how to live if you let it.

Time means nothing to a novel, and it unfolds on its own clock.

The changes in the story you most resist making are the changes (usually) that most need to be made.

A novel is "finished" when it tells you it is. Listen.

Every few months celebrate what you've written.

Writing and completing a novel is a massive undertaking that taxes you physically, emotionally, and intellectually even as you are enlarged by the process. Go to dinner with a friend, treat yourself to a small gift. Writers rarely pat themselves on the back. Learn how to.

4 FEAR IS WHAT YOU FEEL

Fear is often the first thing you feel once you realize or decide that you want to write. I make a distinction between a realization and a decision because they are two vastly different actions. A realization is an intellectual understanding that something is possible –i.e. "I want to write"; a decision is a mind-set that moves you to take action i.e.- "I will write."

I begin this meditation on the writing life with a discussion of the "F" word because it's so hard to acknowledge and produces such a squishy squirmy mix of emotions. You want to write, are often desperate to tell a story. The narrative is throbbing in your heart, keeping you awake at night, has become the sum total of your daydreams. But you can't tell the story because you're scared.

I've been writing with serious intent and the desire to have a public voice since I was a college freshman. Once I decided that I wanted to live and to write "out loud", I wasn't merely frightened of the personal power that would be unleashed if I realized my dream, I was terrified. I was also frightened by the specter of just how much energy and commitment this life I said I wanted to live would require of me.

Over twenty books, and countless articles later I now know the most important thing you need to know about fear-it's an essential part of any creative process. It isn't an emotion you work to "overcome" as much as a type of energy that's a sign that you're about to embark on an adventure and submit yourself to the hearty winds of personal transformation. *You can write often, and with beauty and grace even as you tremble with fear.* You may want to read that last sentence again. *You can write often, and with beauty and grace even as you tremble with fear.*

So, what is it you're afraid of? Well…. There's the fear that you won't write as well as the authors you admire. Fear of ridicule. Fear of the reaction of family and friends. Fear that you can't handle success. Fear that you can't handle failure. Fear that you'll be blinded by the luminosity, the breadth and depth of your talent. Fear of standing up for something because you've seen people who stand up get knocked down. You, like so many of us, have forgotten that "we fall down but we get up."

Winston Churchill said that success is going through failure after failure without losing your enthusiasm. It's the enthusiasm, often difficult to feel and hold onto that ultimately results in the success. Similarly, good writing is essentially draft after draft of fair to middling writing that you "work" until it speaks to the reader in an undeniable way with an unforgettable voice.

Fear can be redefined as an adrenalin rush, a propellant, an ingredient that sets your creativity on fire rather than dousing it. Fear doesn't have to paralyze you unless you're comfortable with it as a cocoon you hide in so you can keep your story to yourself. Your fear cheats the world of another piece of the puzzle that creates the picture of our shared human experience.

I've always known that my desire to be a writer was a gift. Now I know that writing for me, is my assignment from God. *And who I am to talk back to God?* Whether you're a spiritual/religious believer, skeptic, or atheist, it's clear that the urge to create is generated by a source we can't fully know, absolutely define, but only submit to. Therefore, the mystery. Therefore, the wonder. Therefore, the reasons we can't let go of the urge to write.

I conquer fear one word at a time. For me, writing isn't a battle to be won. It's more like a body of water that's alternately murky and crystal clear. It frightens me with rip tides and blustering waves, lulls me on its surface when it is calm, makes music with its rhythmic waltz onto the shore. It cleanses and hypnotizes me. I listen to and dive into it. Some days I swim, others I just float. But I always show up at the beach, and I love the feel of sand between my toes.

5 YOU HAVE TIME TO WRITE

You have time to write. Despite what you think. Despite what you've told yourself. You have time to write. You have the desire and that's the first step in creating the will that launches you into a committed writing life. For writers stymied in their quest to establish a schedule, the issue of time-not enough of it, often becomes a convenient excuse. "If only I had more time," goes the refrain, "I could write more." But you do have more time-24 hours every day from which you can choose some period to write.

Pulitzer-Prize winning author Robert Olen Butler wrote several complete novels commuting to work on the train before his first book was published. Poet Sonia Sanchez wrote at two a.m. when her twin sons were children. I completed the first draft of my memoir *Migrations of the Heart* writing an hour a day at 4 a.m. five days a week for nine months.

You don't have to quit your job to write eight hours a day. You don't have to be the recipient of a grant from the National Endowment for the Arts or a generous MacArthur Genius Award. You just have to write. Half an hour in your journal before you get out of bed in the morning. For fifteen minutes before you go to sleep. The regularity produces results. When I have a large writing project to complete, I break it into small sections and may write as little as half an hour a couple of days a week. I'm still writing however, in the shower, as I wash dishes, when I'm driving, as the narrative gestates in my imagination and continues the process of taking shape. Write **when** you can, **what** you can, **as often** as you can. In a nutshell, that's the secret to writing success.

6 INSPIRATION IS A GOOD PLACE TO START

Inspiration is just the beginning. It's a good place to start, but because of its ephemeral nature, inspiration lacks the ingredients necessary to carry you through to the completion of a writing project or idea. Novice writers often speak rapturously of the power of inspiration, the ability of a mood or feeling to serve as the foundation of their writing life. Yet too often the writing that results from an over reliance on inspiration is infrequently produced and of inconsistent quality. Perhaps the first line or the initial pages blaze like a heady starburst, but the body of the work shows evidence of neglect and even worse, clichés and indifferent writing. Inspiration is designed to provoke in the writer a long-term commitment, not an on again off again infatuation.

Still, the paradoxical nature of this warning is evident. We fall in love with our poems, plays, novels, stories, essays all over again each time we are involved in their creation. Yet the type of love that serves our writing, that ensures its maturation, is love that asks more of us as creators than we think we are capable of. Love that is willing to listen to the story, hear its voice and shove our ego out of the way. Love that imagines our writing on a par with and even surpassing the writing that's moved and inspired us. To reach your goal, always set the bar higher than you think you can reach. You need to be driven and practical, a day dreamer and a doer, in possession of a rich fantasy life and the willingness to work and write and think and imagine page after page even, and especially when you can't see an end in sight.

Inspiration keeps you returning to your writing. It sets you before your computer for an hour before you head to your day-job. Has you writing in your notebook before you drift off to sleep. Allow inspiration to perform its primary task-to place you on the path of consistency. Inspiration is the spark, but hard work is the engine of productivity. Show

up, inspired or not, and the writing will happen, and you will

be inspired by the process you've unleashed.

7 AN AUDIENCE OF ONE

"If I don't tell the truth I lose all interest in writing."
Joyce Carol Oates

Who am I writing for? Who are you? That's a question that's both friend and potential enemy on the path of the writing journey. It's a question that in my earlier days as a writer, I wrestled with often. Was I writing for the imaginary thousands of eager readers who I wanted to buy my books? Was I writing for critics and reviewers, whose opinions are fickle, often biased and that change with the seasons? Maybe I was writing as a way of talking back to all those voices in my head that tried to convince me "Marita face it, you have nothing important to say."

In a sense I write for all those audiences. But I learned rather quickly that most of the time, I was writing for an audience of one, and that audience was me. Powerful writing springs from a solid core of convictions. What do you believe? What are you willing to stand up for even if you must stand up alone? What is your vision of life? Community? Your fellow citizens on the planet? Right? Wrong?

Big questions, yes, but they're the questions whose answers ground you in the essence of the story you render in your writing, exploring its dimensions repeatedly in a variety of ways. Writing is not only lonely, but if you write anything challenging, it's an endeavor that' s guaranteed to spark controversy, get you in "trouble" "offend" someone or leave people puzzled and upset. When I wrote *Don't Play in the Sun One Woman's Journey Through the Color Complex*, about the scourge of intra-racial color discrimination, I was praised and pilloried. Because writing that book allowed me to center myself in an understanding of what I believed about this problem, I could take the hits and the pats on the back almost with equal ease. "But I just want to tell a story, I don't want to change the world", you say. Well, any story you write changes the world. And there are no simple stories. Write about your childhood and your sister will tell you "I don't remember that." Write poetry that rhymes in a free-verse world and people will call you old fashioned and out of touch. Write about what could be and people will assure you it's impossible. Suit up, polish your armor. You said you wanted to write. This is what you signed up for.

I write for me, an audience of one. Yet in my singular existence I'm connected to everyone else. Many of the fictional and nonfiction narratives I've written were conceived to fill what I saw as a void that needed to filled, an absence that had to be addressed. I felt that way deeply and passionately. Those readers who have bought my books confirm that what I felt was merely an echo of a need others saw as well. Writing reminds me again and again how enmeshed we all are in the fabric of each other's dreams and desires. There are only a few major themes that most stories dramatize or address-family, love, the desire to be safe, identity, guilt, redemption. If I'm creating characters or offering new ideas about any of those themes, I'm inevitably connected to and a reflection of everyone else on earth. That's why great literature is so effective at smashing through the walls and barriers we constantly erect to divide us one from another.

The writers who've provided the model for my writing life have marched to the beat of their own drum and turned their stories into an instrument that created new ways of looking at the familiar. The writers I admire write from the inside out, from the center of who they are, not who others tell them they should be. These are writers willing to risk telling a story the world is not yet ready to hear. They know the world will only become ready for the story if they tell it.

Writing is serious business and serious writing forces the writer, of necessity, to become their own best friend. The garden of private fantasies is the soil from which the amazing and the beautiful constantly springs. Get to know your audience of one. Make sure she has a front row seat.

8 EIGHT THINGS WRITERS DO

Writers Write. No excuses. On a schedule. With regularity.

Writers Read. The writers working in their genre. The writers in other genres, so they can learn something new and maintain a fresh perspective on the many different ways stories are told.

Writers Write. And they seek out constructive assessment of their work from smart readers whose opinions and instincts they trust.

Writers Attend Public Readings by other writers, poetry slams, book signings, lectures, to support other writers and to form a community they can learn from. Writers take workshops and classes to hone their craft.

Writers Write. And they revise, revise, revise; edit, change, alter, re-imagine, all in the service of telling the best story the best way they can.

Writers cheer the success of other writers. So that they don't block their own blessings. Writers realize success is a state of mind they control and define, not something given to them by anyone else.

Writers Practice Patience. A story has its own deadline, its own schedule. The timeline you designed is just a joke that makes God laugh! Expect frustration, surprises, disappointment, unexpected detours as your story struggles to be born.

Writers Write. Yes, they do. Yes, you can.

9 EVERYTHING IS EVERYTHING

The decision to write is about much more than just writing regularly, even though that's where you'll start. You're creating a new life and lifestyle. In this endeavor, everything counts, or as we used to say (I'm showing my age here) *"everything is everything."*

The decision to write can have a quake-like effect in your life. An earthquake shifts the earths' crust, shaking and cracking it, releasing a powerful blast of energy that while a natural and normal act of nature, leaves destruction in its wake. Think of the energy released in your life by the decision to write, as an earthquake in reverse, one that builds rather than destroys.

Once you begin writing with serious intent, that action will inevitably shift your priorities, and result in displacements and replacements in the major areas of your life. When the dust settles, you'll gaze upon a life-scape different from the one you once knew. Expect these shifts in the major areas of your life and define them as opportunities for growth.

- **Family** If you're married with children or living with a partner, once you've decided to give more time to developing your writing, talk with these most important people in your life. Tell them why you've made this decision and what it means to you. Honestly discuss the trade-offs that will be required, i.e. rather than snuggling on the sofa to watch TV every evening with your partner, you may need to spend that time writing. This can be an opportunity to encourage greater self-reliance in children and partners. Enlist the people you live with as your cheering squad. Let them know that more money could result from your writing which would help everyone; you'll be more content, devoting regular time to an activity you enjoy and that will affect them as well. Let them know that they remain important and it's because they are that you need their support.

- **Friends/Family** Giving yourself permission to write can sometimes inspire an unsettling, unexpected emotional backlash from friends and even family, who may wonder or even ask *"Who told you you could write?"* Long-festering, buried resentments, jealousies, even anger can erupt in the face of your decision to act on behalf of your creative power. While you can't replace disgruntled, fearful family members, you can find new friends who can support your creative life. If you suspect that divulging the "great news" (from your perspective) that you're writing will encourage these negative reactions, hold onto your dream in silence.

- **Physical/Mental Health** Writing is taskmaster, buddy, interloper, and friend. The writing life is also demanding and sometimes grueling. You write with your mind and imagination, and with your body. Stretch frequently when writing on the computer, take periodic ten-minute breaks that give your eyes a rest from the screen. Practice yoga or Pilates work out in the gym. The healthier and more fit you are, the more productive your writing life will be. Don't let writing take over your life. Make time for friends, fun and family. Laugh often and develop a sense of humor, believe me you'll need it.

- **Work** The more time you commit to writing, the more you may be tempted to see your 9-5 job as irrelevant and intrusive. When I worked a 9 to 5, I woke up early to get a start on my day and to perform what were for me the most important rituals of my day. I'd pray, then meditate and do half an hour of yoga, followed by an hour of writing. Having written for an hour before the onslaught of the demands of the day, I could go to work and feel much less resentment toward work that paid the rent but that didn't have my heart. Be grateful for your job. A check you can depend on provides you with the cushion you rely on to write. While I don't advocate remaining on a job that's killing your spirit, a job doesn't have to be an obstacle to the writing life, unless you define it as such.

- **Faith** If you never prayed before you began writing, you will once you become deeply entrenched in this endeavor. The rigors of the commitment you've made will sometimes test your faith in yourself, impatience with the process will have you in dark moods muttering, *"what have I gotten myself into?"*. You'll be afraid that if you don't hurry and complete your project there won't be any success left in the world for you. Be assured, the universe isn't stingy and there really is an inexhaustible supply of potential and possibilities. Buddhist meditation, silent retreats, my belief in an indwelling divinity, the love and support of my husband, family and friends reinforces my faith. Each time I sit down to write, that act alone affirms my faith in myself. The words come as an eager response to my own belief. Find the spiritual tools that work for you, that keep you spiritually grounded so you can soar.

10 THE TRUTH ABOUT MONEY

Money. It's another topic, like fear, that haunts (quite literally) the lives of writers. Some writers are unabashed in their willingness to acknowledge their desire to become rich and famous (mostly rich). Even the most idealistic writer, one more focused on the perfect sentence than the bottom line, hopes to make a profit from their work. The great American poet Walt Whitman and the iconic writer Ernest Hemingway were both brazen, often brilliant self-promoters, who cared deeply about craft, getting paid the value of their work *and* a lasting literary legacy. So, an interest in money is not inconsistent with a commitment to good writing. Money isn't dirty, or evil and it won't corrupt you unless you're ready to be corrupted. Besides, writers are like everybody else. We want to get paid.

How much money do writers make? It varies. Beginning poets are, unfortunately, often paid next to nothing, sometimes receiving only a set number of copies of their book on publication, until the book begins selling. Children's book authors are higher on the scale, but they don't generally get sizeable advances. It takes years to become a Judy Blume or Eloise Greenfield. Self-published authors bear the entire financial burden of publication and promotion, and very few self-published authors are prepared for the challenges of the enterprise or fully recover their financial investment. A first-time author of a literary fiction or nonfiction book could get $50,000 or more as an advance from a major publisher. Expect half that amount from a smaller publishing house. If the writer is incredibly lucky and publishers fall in love with the book the size of the advance can go into six figures or more. Writing about a controversial person or topic can also increase the amount of the advance. If you're a free-lance writer, a reputable national magazine pays a dollar per word for your published story.

How do writers get their money? After your agent has negotiated a contract on your behalf, they receive 25% of the advance. The advance is the amount of money a publisher gives you to write the book and is often broken down into three payments. One on signing the contract. One on completion of the manuscript. And the final payment upon publication of the book. In tabulating this income, writers often forget that they're required to pay taxes on the advance. That $50,000 is shrinking fast, isn't it?

Royalties are profits earned by a writer after the publisher has recouped the advance plus other costs related to the production and promotion of the book. My advances have ranged from $10,000 (my first advance in 1980), to$130,000 for my book *Saving Our Sons Raising Black Children in a Turbulent World.*

Yet the largest royalty check I've ever received is $2,000.00. My agent, who has represented me for forty years, told me in our first conversation, that she wanted to work with me over the long haul, the highs and lows of my career and that money was not the most important reason to choose a publisher. Finding a good editor who could encourage and demand my best writing and a publishing house that valued and respected my unique voice were what she would look for in protecting my interests as her client.

So how does a writer live comfortably off their writing? By selling hundreds of thousands or millions of copies of a book. By living off the royalties from those sales, which become a passive form of income the writer can rely on.

This doesn't mean that you can't become a writer who lives the writer's fantasy life. Enterprising writers *can* get paid. The books I've written have provided me with advances, royalties and a reputation that has garnered me lucrative speaking engagements and writing assignments all over the world. My training as a journalist allows me to write for magazines, even as I'm allowing a novel to percolate. I teach writing workshops, deliver lectures and readings; I offer editing and literary coaching services. Because I write both nonfiction and fiction, I have more options as a writer than if I had mastered only one genre. Early in my career, the desire to provide my young son with a materially "good" life of options and opportunities was a huge source of the drive that energized my career and made it so productive. The success I've attained isn't exactly the success I dreamed of, in many ways it's even better. The final truth about money is that there's plenty out there, but even the most financially successful writer is motivated to write largely because they love telling stories, it's that simple. Yes. Do what you love, and the money will come.

11 HONOR YOUR TRIBE

When I realized that writing was both my calling and my career it became important for me to live in an environment where I could find a community of Black writers. I was living in Boston when I committed to the writer's life, and increasingly disheartened by the racial fragmentation and tension in the city, and the absence at that time of a meaningful Black writing community, I headed back to my hometown, Washington, D.C. When I returned, I found a vibrant and active group of Black writers-poets, journalists, novelists who met regularly and had numerous informal support groups. Without this cadre of writer/friends I'd been lonely, felt adrift and unsure. What I found offered me much needed fellowship. It also inspired me to become a literary activist, founding first the African American Writers Guild and several years later the Zora Neale Hurston/Richard Wright Foundation.

For over thirty years working through both those organizations, I labored on behalf of my fellow writers to create more and better opportunities for growth, recognition, and community for Black writers. During those years when I worked diligently for other writers, my own career blossomed. Everything I worked to provide for my fellow writers came in abundance to me. I think somehow the two are connected.

My fellow writers have as no others in my life, understood the journey of the writing life. They've provided me with valuable and constructive criticism of my work and welcome and much appreciated praise. Together we've bemoaned the travails of the publishing world and celebrated each other's successes. A really good book by a writer I know and call a friend, or even a writer that I don't know but admire, is an inspiration to me to write as well or better-that's healthy competition. Only another writer knows how it feels to be "blocked" or can appreciate the strange mix of gratitude and frustration you feel signing a new book and being asked by the person who just bought it "So when is your next one coming out?" Only another writer knows that you had to give almost everything to get *this one* done. Only another writer understands how good it can feel to have a fictional character come to life on the page after years of struggling to hear her voice and capture it on the page.

One of the best ways I've gained a full sense of the complexities and challenges and rewards of the writers' life is to read the autobiographies, biographies, and journals of writers. Reading John Steinbeck's *Working Days: The Journals of The Grapes of Wrath* I learned how all writers must create amid the onslaught of the messy and unpredictable requirements of daily life.

Zora Neale Hurston's memoir *Dust Tracks on a Road* gave me an appreciation for her zest for living, her courage and love of adventure and to see how that informed her stories. When I read the journals of abolitionist and poet Henry David Thoreau, I found a spiritual soul mate and experienced with a stunning precision the beauty of nature, breathing on the page. Richard Wright's *Black Boy* is a meditation on how his childhood of poverty was a metaphor for children of poverty everywhere.

When I think of my writing community, my tribe, I claim the living and the dead, and writers of all races and ethnicities. Wherever we are, we are the keepers of the powerful flame of the story. We are lauded and praised, jailed, and tortured for the stories and the truths we tell. Science fiction writer Ursula K. Le Guin has said, "The story… is one of the basic tools invented by the human mind for the purpose of understanding. There have been great societies that did not use the wheel, but there have been no societies that did not tell stories." We are the stories we tell.

Honor the members of your tribe by buying their books, joining organizations that support the professional and political endeavors we engage in, and by adding your writers' vision and voice to the circle of stories, a circle that must not be broken.

"A diary necessarily has no form beyond the accidental one of improvisation and hence though it cannot be a work or art... perhaps it can be a masterpiece."
Jean Paul Sartre

12 PUBLISH OR PERISH?

What if you don't want to publish? What if you just want to write in a journal or keep a diary? Is that writing valuable too? Journal writing by its very nature and intent is therapeutic. Writing in a journal can resurrect the spirit and become a source of continual emotional rebirth. A journal keeps your secrets, and it doesn't talk back.

The act of writing launches you on a restructuring and a remembering process about the past and allows you to envision the future in delicious solitude. When I journal, I think of the writing on those pages as a first draft of my future. On the pages of my journal I admit, confess, worry, celebrate, and congratulate myself with more honesty than anywhere else.

For some writers, the journal becomes the place where story ideas evolve and mature over time, where they build up the courage to write for others as well as themselves.

The dialogue between you and the pages of a journal possesses a sacred quality because the revelations, the longing expressed, the fears exposed, come unadulterated, shot straight from the heart. All writing for the public is a kind of performance. You write with an eye on both the story and its intended audience.

A journal is a resting place where your thoughts and feelings are perfect just as they are. There are pitifully few other places where you will be met with so much generosity and absence of judgment as on the pages of a journal. A journal greets you with an open invitation every day and it says, come as you are. Be what you are. There is nothing you can say or reveal that will make me turn away.

13 WHY YOUR STORY MATTERS

One of the joys of teaching writing is that I get to stay connected to people, their passions, their energy, and their possibilities. I've been teaching writing for many years, and no matter who or where I teach, writing workshops and classes are where people come to be enlarged. When you enroll in a writers' workshop you may think that it's just because you want to learn how to write. I think you're taking my class because you want to reinvigorate a hibernating imagination, give voice to a long-closeted and insistent narrative, leave the safety of the shore. Life is at its essence about evolution and change. That's what writing is about too.

I'm renewed by the stories my students share, and each class of writers teaches me how to teach them, how to listen, and how to honor what they are sharing. When you take a writing class, you're signing on to stand butt naked before strangers. To willingly submit your work and your ideas to the assessment of people you've never met, don't know and after the class may never see again. And you do this trusting that somehow you will not only survive this process but thrive as a result.

You're enrolled in a writing class also because you know instinctively that your story matters. Scientists have concluded that because of quantum physics we are, all us, literally connected to one another through energy. We keep trying to divide and conquer our individual souls. But that is a battle that can't be won. We are connected. That's why a war fought thousands of miles away from where we live causes us such anguish, it's why a story set in a foreign land speaks to us as though it was unfolding in our mother tongue.

Your story matters because, it's my story. Your story matters because I'm not complete without it. Often in my classes and workshops students enroll clearly because they have a need to write from the perspective of one who has been traditionally marginalized by society. When I work with writers who are gay or lesbian, or has felt diminished because of their gender identity, racial or color discrimination, sexual or physical abuse, I urge them to write about and from the core of this sense of marginalization. They have a duty, I tell them, to take me as a reader to that place, the place where our souls can be joined.

Often the writing we produce that is inspired by anger, or a desire to right a wrong has an awe-inspiring quality. It's the honesty of the writing that makes it shimmer with eloquence. But we need to write out of a sense of joy too. Writing is often associated with suffering some even see writing itself as a form of punishment. We need to write to celebrate ourselves, our struggles, what we have achieved and what we have *tried* to achieve. Yes, writing well is a challenge, but every sentence I write and then re-write is a celebration of myself, my imagination, and my tenacity.

All stories are true (for someone) and all stories matter. Giving the world your story, even if and especially, if it hurts, or is a story everyone said no one would believe, is an act of altruism woven into the fabric of our everyday miracle life. You do not have to make your story matter. It already does.

.

14 THE POWER OF THE PROMPT

A prompt is a sentence or passage that is designed to jump-start your imagination and your writing process. I use prompts in my writing workshops. When working on my projects I create prompts customized for the story I am writing. Prompts are invaluable as a spur to diving deep into a character or a story. I find that often prompts work best when they are timed. When you know that you have five minutes, ten minutes, or fifteen minutes to write, you turn off your censors, and you mute the internal critic because you want to write and you don't have time to waste. In this concluding section, I share prompts that will support your discovery of story, character, themes, and the internal truth of your story.

Memoir is a genre dear to my heart. I launched my writing career as a published author with my memoir *Migrations of the Heart.* We love memoirs because we love "true stories" of others that connect them to us and our experience. One of the most under-utilized techniques for emerging/beginning writers is narrative. Narrative is telling, explaining, but powerful narrative reveals the story and the character in ways that evoke an emotional response in the reader. A response that makes it impossible to stop reading. In writing your memoir you must convince that reader that you have told them everything, that no secret has been left untold. I have never written a memoir in which I shared *everything,* but it was important that the reader feel I had. The prompts that follow have been designed for memoir but can be used to discover and rediscover any story, no matter its form.

My most powerful childhood memory is of _____

because it captures all the _____ I felt then

and sometimes feel now.

To vividly describe my father, I have to tell you about his

_____.

It was my mother's _____ that told you

everything you needed to know about her.

When I discovered my father's _____ it

changed everything I had thought about him.

My mother's friends were the kind of women who

_____.

My childhood home made me feel _____.

When I turned _____ and got my

_____ I finally felt _____.

My favorite sibling was _____ because when I

was _____ they _____.

My most important teacher in school taught me that I was

_____.

Ours was a family of secrets, and the most painful one was

_____.

As a child I loved _____ because when I

was _____ I was _____.

My childhood neighborhood was populated by memorable

"characters", men and women like _____.

My grandmother was a _____ to me.

The most important thing my parents gave me as a child

was _____.

My grandfather was a _____ to me.

I betrayed a good friend when I _____.

When my mother gave me the gift of

_____ I knew she understood me.

My father treated me like _____.

Only now that I am a woman do I understand why mother

_____.

When I lost _____ I thought I had lost

everything until _____.

My favorite fictional character is _____

because _____.

The job that nearly killed my spirit was _____.

I was afraid to express anger and so _____.

I was afraid to express love and so _____.

Eight pm on a summer night on my childhood street

looked like _____ and sounded like

_____.

We were a church-going family and that meant

_____.

Cards, liquor, and music that was the recipe for a good time

in _____.

I was a _____ child and felt

comfortable _____.

When I _____ and looked in the mirror at myself

I finally felt free.

**

Fiction as an endeavor is both demanding and exhilarating. The following prompts provide an opportunity to use scenes, dialogue, and narrative in response to the storyline. While I use the gender identifying pronouns, she/he these are your prompts so adapt them as you desire. Each prompt asks that you write in response either a narrative (telling, explaining, recreating), or a scene with dialogue.

When I opened the door and saw them, my first impulse was to _____ but then I_____.

Narrative

For the first time in his life, he wanted to tell them what he believed, and so he just blurted out _____.

Scene

If the town she grew up in was a color, that color would be

_____ because it captured the town's _____.

Narrative

They sat like that for the longest time, exchanging one or

two- word sentences that said much more than it seemed.

Scene

Describe a scene of sexual pleasure alternating points of

view of those in the scene.   Narrative

All six of us stood around the cemetery plot as daddy's

casket was lowered into the ground and that's when

Alice_____. Scene

I stood apart from the others, remembering

_____. Narrative

"You're lying" Jason shouted and then

I_____. Scene

For month after the funeral, she dreamed about daddy,

dreams that_____. Narrative

My sister was dying and finally, things felt alright between

us. There wasn't much to say and so I _____.

Scene

He had always hated his brother and loved him in equal

measure, because_____. Narrative

We disagreed about everything including what happened

that night. Scene

Standing before what was left of their house after the

hurricane Jason thought and felt _____.

Narrative

You Don't Know Me (Yet) A Biography of Your Character

Provide the following information about your character to get to know them.

Astrological Sign

Favorite Color

Major emotional strength

Major emotional weakness

Biggest Secret

Who have they never forgiven?

Favorite Subject in School

Occupation

Relationship with Mother

Relationship with Father

Relationship with Siblings

Sexually active?

Who do they envy?

Which political party do they belong to?

Do they have any fears about money?

Dream job

Would they make the first move to start a relationship?

Are they active on social media?

Favorite singer, musician, or music group

Who do they admire in their personal life?

What public figure do they admire?

What do they believe they could never do?

How does your character want to be remembered after

they die?

"Whenever my environment had failed to support or nourish me, I had clutched at books..."
Richard Wright, Black Boy

BOOKS BY MARITA GOLDEN

- *A Miracle Every Day: Triumph and Transformation in the Lives of Single Mothers*
- *A Woman's Place*
- *After*
- *And Do Remember Me*
- *Don't Play in the Sun: One Woman's Journey Through the Color Complex*
- *First Page to Finished On Writing and the Writer's Life*
- *Gumbo: An Anthology of African-American Writing*
- *It's All Love: Black Writers on Soul Mates, Family and Friends*
- *Long Distance Life*
- *Migrations of the Heart*
- *Saving Our Sons: Raising Black Children in a Turbulent World*
- *Skin Deep: Black and White Women Write About Race*
- *The Edge of Heaven*
- *The New Black Woman Loves Herself Has Boundaries Heals Every Day*
- *The Strong Black Woman How a Myth Endangers the Physical and Mental Health of Black Women*
- *The Wide Circumference of Love*
- *The Word: Black Writers Talk About the Transformative Power of Reading and Writing*
- *Us Against Alzheimer's: Stories of Family, Love and Faith*
- *Wild Woman Don't Wear No Blues: Black Women Writers on Love, Men and Sex*
- *What Every Black Parent Needs to Know About Saving Our Sons Institutionalized Racism and Raising Black Children*
- *Skin An Interactive Journal for Women Who Want to Heal The Color Complex*

ABOUT THE AUTHOR

Marita Golden is the author of over twenty works of fiction and nonfiction that include the memoir *Migrations of the Heart* and the novels *After,* and *The Wide Circumference of Love.* She served on the MFA Creative Writing faculties at George Mason University and Virginia Commonwealth University, and as Visiting Distinguished Writer at Johns Hopkins University and The University of the District of Columbia. She is co-founder and President Emerita of the Zora Neale Hurston/Richard Wright Foundation. She has received recognition for her writing from the Association of Maryland Librarians, the Black Caucus of the American Library Association, and the International Hall of Fame of Writers of African Descent. Her literary activism has been honored with a Distinguished Service Award from the Authors Guild, and the Barnes and Noble Writers for Writers Award presented by *Poets and Writers.*

For more information on Marita Golden visit her website maritagolden.com.

www.ingramcontent.com/pod-product-compliance
Lightning Source LLC
LaVergne TN
LVHW052038080426
835513LV00018B/2379